BERKSHIRE
PUB WALKS

Alex Milne-White

COUNTRYSIDE BOOKS
NEWBURY BERKSHIRE

First published 2019
© 2019 Alex Milne-White

All rights reserved. No part of this publication may be reproduced,
stored in a retrieval system, or transmitted by any means,
electronic, mechanical, photocopying, recording or otherwise,
without the prior written permission of the copyright
holder and publishers.

COUNTRYSIDE BOOKS
3 Catherine Road
Newbury, Berkshire

To view our complete range of books,
please visit us at
www.countrysidebooks.co.uk

ISBN 978 1 84674 389 4

All materials used in the manufacture of this book carry FSC certification

Produced through The Letterworks Ltd., Reading
Designed and typeset by KT Designs, St Helens
Printed by Holywell Press, Oxford

CONTENTS

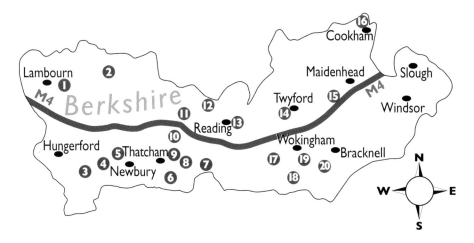

PUBLISHER'S NOTE

We hope that you obtain considerable enjoyment from this book; great care has been taken in its preparation. Although at the time of publication all routes followed public rights of way or permitted paths, diversion orders can be made and permissions withdrawn.

We cannot, of course, be held responsible for such diversion orders and any inaccuracies in the text which result from these or any other changes to the routes, nor any damage which might result from walkers trespassing on private property. We are anxious though that all the details covering the walks are kept up to date and would therefore welcome information from readers which would be relevant to future editions.

The simple sketch maps that accompany the walks in this book are based on notes made by the author whilst checking out the routes on the ground. They are designed to show you how to reach the start, to point out the main features of the overall circuit, and they contain a progression of numbers that relate to the paragraphs of the text.

However, for the benefit of a proper map, we do recommend that you purchase the relevant Ordnance Survey sheet covering your walk. Ordnance Survey maps are widely available, especially through booksellers and local newsagents.

INTRODUCTION

The Royal County of Berkshire is exquisitely and quintessentially English. Rolling hills and lush farmland hide innumerable pretty villages and a host of top-class pubs, from the traditional to the modern. With the Wessex Downs to the west, the mighty River Thames snaking along its north-eastern border, Berkshire was almost tailor-made for the pub walk enthusiast.

All of which made the task of choosing the very best pub walks in the county a difficult one. Somehow we managed it. The walks you'll find here are mostly in the region of 4 miles, with a few of them coming in a mile or so shorter or longer. This makes them just about ideal for working up an appetite for a pub lunch - or burning off the calories if you decide to eat beforehand. These are pubs I know personally, so I can vouch for the quality of the food and service.

The gentle landscape of the North Wessex Downs might not present the same physical challenge as somewhere like the Lake District fells, but caution is still required wherever you go walking. Check the weather forecast before setting off and dress accordingly, choose appropriate footwear and stick to the map. There are sketch maps for each walk here. If you plan to deviate from the route, make sure you have an OS map with you as well.

I have tried to give some indication of how likely some walks are to be muddy, but you won't need me to tell you how difficult our Great British weather makes it to predict these things accurately. As a general rule of thumb, paths in wooded areas can get pretty muddy at most times of the year.

I hope you enjoy these walks as much as I loved putting them together.

Alex

Walk 1
EAST GARSTON

Distance: 4 miles (6.4 km)

Map: OS Explorer 158 Newbury & Hungerford
Grid Ref: SU366764

How to get there: From junction 14 of the M4 head north towards Wantage. After a couple of miles the road bends sharp left through Great Shefford, turn left opposite the pub and continue for another 1½ miles where the first building you will see in East Garston is the Queens Arms. The car park is just beyond the pub on the main road. **Sat Nav:** RG17 7ET.

Parking: The pub has quite a large car park but please ask permission if you aren't planning to visit before or after your walk.

Berkshire Pub Walks

This walk follows a pleasant path alongside the River Lambourn, followed by a steady climb up to some lovely views across the Lambourn Downs and a stroll through the pretty village of East Garston to finish – all in all a very pleasant walk.

**THE
PUB** **THE QUEENS ARMS** is an award-winning, attractive, vibrant and recently-restored pub and hotel. It has a large (and dog-friendly) bar, a restaurant, a covered patio area and a large garden. Lunch is served every day and dinner every day except Sunday, when there's a pizza oven fired up until 8pm. Bar snacks are also available.
🌐 queensarmseastgarston.co.uk ☎ 01488 648757

The Walk

1 Turn right out of the **Queens Arms car park** along the grass verge and then turn right following the purple footpath arrow down a narrow path that opens onto a gravel driveway. Cross the bridge over the river and turn right onto the road. After less than 100 metres go straight on. When the road turns, follow the sign for **Lambourn Valley Way**. At a junction of paths keep straight on next to the **River Lambourn**.

2 Stay on this pleasant riverside path for about ½ mile. Go through a wooden kissing gate, past some weeping willow trees to a lane. Turn left on the lane, following a byway sign up to **Maidencourt Farm**, and continue straight on up a wide track. Continue up the hill and you will see a public footpath sign pointing left after about 500 metres (which would take you straight back to East Garston), carry on up the hill and shortly after you've reached the top of the hill you will see an Ordnance Survey triangulation station on the left and a footpath sign pointing right, but again carry straight on.

3 Eventually the path dog-legs to the left a little. Shortly after that you can see a signpost marking a junction of a byway and public bridleway, turn sharp left here onto the bridleway down the hill. This narrow path can be a little muddy and gets churned up by many hooves so watch your footing. Follow the path down to a road and turn right (turning left would be another short cut back to East Garston) for about 200 metres, then left onto an un-signposted lane.

4 Keep straight on as the lane turns into a narrower path, then after about 500 metres you will see a large open gate on the left with a yellow footpath arrow. Follow this path down the hill, dog-legging slightly left, and then up the other side. If you look left and back at this point you can see most of the last couple of miles of the route. Just before a paddock the path bears right with a stile going straight on, go over the stile following the footpath arrow down to a junction of paths.

5 Go straight on down towards the village, and again at another junction, down

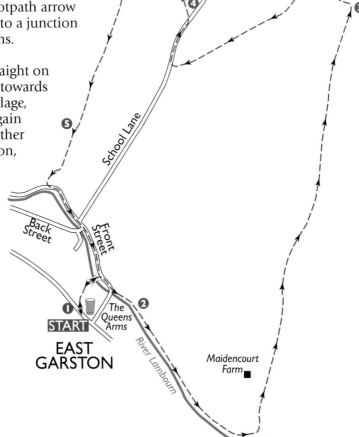

to the road that runs through **East Garston**. Turn left along the road, passing a number of pretty thatched cottages and keeping the river on your right, until you see a purple arrow pointing right, over the bridge you crossed earlier. Follow the path back up to the pub and as you reach it you may notice a short cut into the car park.

Places of Interest

East Garston is in the heart of 'The Valley of the Racehorse' with the River Lambourn flowing through the middle and rolling downland on either side. It's a pretty village, with lots of thatched cottages, and it even has its own music festival 'Garstonbury'; a mixture of tribute acts and local bands. There's plenty of good walking in the area as long as you don't mind a bit of a climb, or if you stick to the Lambourn Valley Way it's only about 2km to **Eastbury**, another pretty village with a great pub, the Eastbury Plough, at the heart of it.

Walk 2
EAST ILSLEY

Distance: 5¾ miles (9 km)

Map: OS Explorer 170 Vale of White Horse **Grid Ref:** SU493812

How to get there: From the M4 take the A34 north and after about 5 minutes you will see a sign for East Ilsley. Drive into the village and you will see the Crown & Horns opposite the Swan. **Sat Nav:** RG20 7LH.

Parking: The pub has its own car park for patrons, or there are some on-street parking spaces further along the road.

This is one of the longer walks in the book, but is well worth the extra effort for the views of the lovely countryside, rolling downs and pretty villages. Racehorses are trained up on the downs and you might well see them galloping past next to the Ridgeway if you're lucky. Racehorses have been trained at East Ilsley for about 200 years. The Harrow in West Ilsley is a very popular and well regarded pub so if you need refreshments two thirds of the way around head to the far end of West Ilsley and pop in.

THE PUB THE CROWN & HORNS is a cosy country inn, which has been refurbished and renovated with oak beams and log fires for colder months and a courtyard for warmer ones. The menu is a mixture of pub classics mixed with some more imaginative dishes, plus pizzas and sandwiches or roasts on a Sunday.
⊕ crownandhorns.com ☎ 01635 281545

The Walk

1 From the pub car park turn right onto **Compton Road** and then turn left to stay on **Compton Road**. After 100 metres you will see a public footpath signpost with four options – take the footpath that goes hard left between some houses and a fence. At the end of this path turn right onto a public bridleway taking you up

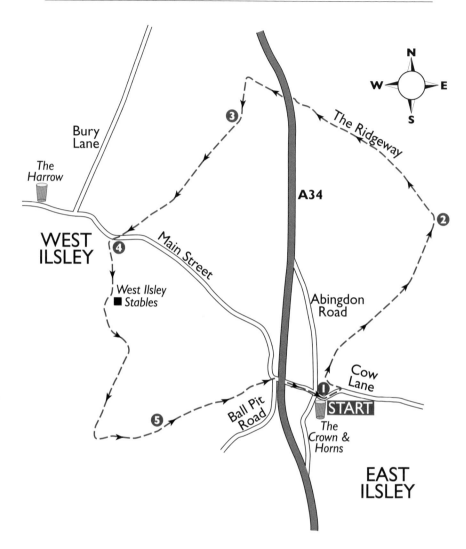

onto the downs. At the end of the bridleway cross straight over the gallop track and then left onto the **Ridgeway**.

2 Stay on the wide path, past a couple of turnings on the left, and keep straight on at a junction of paths. At a second junction of paths, just before the A34, turn right to stay on the **Ridgeway** as it passes through a tunnel under the road and back uphill on the other side. Keep going straight on for about 100 metres then turn left on a restricted byway, passing some more racehorse gallops on your left.

3 When you reach a fork in the path, keep right on the byway as it turns into a pleasant tree-lined path heading down towards **West Ilsley**. At the bottom of the hill, shortly after a path joins from the right, turn right onto a road, then almost immediately turn left onto a small road signed to **West Ilsley Stables** (unless you want to visit **The Harrow** for a well earned rest, in which case follow the main road through the village to the other end). Ignore footpaths heading right and bear left onto a road, signposted as a public bridleway.

4 Stay on the road until you see a public bridleway sign pointing right, follow the path past a metal gate, then turn left onto a broad track. At a junction of paths turn left, then immediately right, staying on the bridleway as it goes up the hill. Follow a track around to the right and then down the hill to a junction of footpaths. Turn left onto a tree-lined path and shortly after, turn left again. Another path branches left after about 100 metres, but stay straight on.

5 Follow this track (called **Woolvers Road**) up onto the downs with great views of West Ilsley, the downs, and much of the route you have just covered, then head down towards the A34 and join the road to go under it. Keep going straight along the pavement until you reach your starting point.

Places of Interest

The Ridgeway is an 87-mile long national trail that has been used since prehistoric times by travellers, herdsmen and soldiers. It is said to be Britain's oldest road. It starts at Overton Hill near Avebury in Wiltshire and mainly sticks to the higher ground, on chalk downland, all the way to Ivinghoe Beacon, in the Chiltern Hills, in Hertfordshire.

Because of East Ilsley's position on the Ridgeway and other ancient routes it became the centre of a great corn market in the middle ages. Later the growing wool trade turned it into a famous sheep market, to which James I gave royal approval in 1620. This became the second largest sheep market throughout the 19th century, after Smithfield in London, and there were apparently 24 inns and public houses to cater for the hordes of farmers and shepherds on market day.

Walk 3
INKPEN

Distance: 5 miles (8 km)

Map: OS Explorer 158 Newbury & Hungerford
Grid Ref: SU378638

How to get there: Do not drive into Inkpen and expect to happen across the right place, Inkpen is not a village in the sense that most people would understand it. It's more a string of houses and farms connected by a network of small winding roads. The easiest way to get to the Crown & Garter is to take the A4 from Newbury towards Hungerford and follow signs to Kintbury. In the middle of Kintbury turn left, opposite the newsagents, and follow this road for about 2 miles until you reach the pub. **Sat Nav: RG17 9QR.**

Parking: The pub has a car park at the rear, but be sure to use the pub or café if you park there.

This walk is a little longer than some in the book, and a bit more energetic too, but it is well worth it for the lovely scenery along the way and the fine views across the downs. Combe

Gibbet (see Places of Interest) is an impressive sight up on the hill and unless it's a completely windless day you will probably see paragliders launching themselves off the slopes near the gibbet. You will also pass Walbury Hill which, at 297 metres above sea level, is the highest natural point in South East England. You can cut about 1km off the walk by walking straight up the hill at point 4, but be warned, it's a steep path!

THE CROWN & GARTER is an award-winning, country pub with great food. There is a large and pretty beer garden on one side of the pub and a café on the other. They are both part of the Honesty Group, set up by local chef Romilla Arber, which also has a cookery school near Newbury and a small string of cafés. As the name suggests Honesty is all about the customer knowing where their food has come from and using integrity in the food chain. The menu is therefore full of delicious local and seasonal produce at fair prices.

⊕ crownandgarter.co.uk ☎ 01488 668325

The Walk

1 From the car park take the track behind the pub, heading away from the road. After about 200 metres you will come to

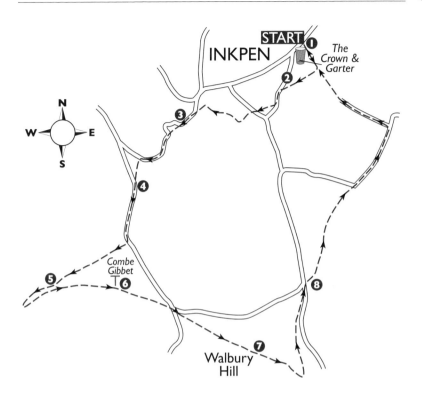

a junction, turn right in the direction of the public footpath sign along the left edge of the field. Halfway along the field you will see a wooden kissing gate with a yellow footpath arrow, go through the gate and carry on in the same direction through a small orchard.

② Cross the track leading to a house, then go through a kissing gate onto a road and turn left. After 50 metres follow the public footpath sign forking off to the right. Cross over another road and go through a kissing gate into a field. Bear slightly right, towards the right corner of the field, and go through another kissing gate and then along the left edge of the field. Shortly after the field curves to the right, follow a yellow footpath arrow directing you through a gate onto a muddy bit of field, then along to the next gate and straight on and along to a small road. Ignore the various footpath signs and head left on the road.

3 As the road starts to bear right you will see a footpath sign pointing left, follow the direction of the sign straight across a field and then back onto the road again, and turn left. Follow this narrow, windy and little-used road for about 350 metres until you see an obvious footpath sign pointing left. Again follow the direction of the sign straight across a field (the path may not be clear), in the direction of **Combe Gibbet** up on the hill, and down to a gap in the hedge leading onto another road.

4 Turn left on the road and carry on until just after the road bends, where you will see a footpath arrow pointing right. Follow this past a superfluous stile and then over another stile. There are two paths here; the shallower path to the right is the course of this walk, but if you're short of time and/or feeling energetic you can take the path straight up the hill to the gibbet, which cuts about 1km off the walk, and rejoin the walk at point 6. If not, take the less steep path gradually up the hill. As you near the top, the path will become less clear but keep heading in the same direction, through the middle of a clump of scrubby bushes, until you reach the top of the hill.

5 Bear slightly right on a clearer path near a fence and carry on until you come to a gate, with a blue public bridleway arrow nearby, on your left. Go through the gate and bear right towards a large metal gate, go through this gate onto a wide track and turn left. Follow this track towards the gibbet until shortly before it you see a gate on the left. Go through the gate and walk up to the gibbet.

6 Walk down to a metal gate on the other side to rejoin the wide track and head down to a road. Go straight over onto a smaller road, and then bear right on the byway just before car park. The path forks after about 200 metres and you can take either fork as they rejoin later. Stay on the path as it ascends slightly until you reach the highest point of the walk next to **Walbury Hill**. There is a gate and a sort of stile on the right along here. You can cross over onto **Walbury Hill** and to the actual highest point, where there is a stone triangulation pillar, but then return to the path.

7 Stay on the track until you see a clear footpath sign pointing both left and right. Follow the left arrow over a stile and bear slightly left onto a faint path across the field. The path becomes clearer as you head towards and past a defunct stile. Walk along the ridge until you see a wooden stile. Cross over the stile onto a winding path through a copse. At the end of the path cross a small road onto a public footpath through another copse and to the corner of a large field.

8 Turn left along the left edge of the field, being careful of the electric fence, all the way down to the bottom corner of the field. Then, turn right briefly and then left through a gap in the fence onto a road. Head straight on along the opposite road past the sign for **West Woodhay**. Ignore the footpath on your left after about 250 metres. After another 250 metres turn left on the lane/byway. Follow the lane as it eventually turns into a track and walk straight on all the way back to the pub's car park.

Places of Interest

Combe Gibbet, on Gallows Down, was erected in 1676 for the purpose of gibbeting the bodies of George Broomham and Dorothy Newman, who were having an affair and were hanged for murdering George's wife and son after they discovered them together on the downs. The gibbet was placed in such a prominent location as a warning to deter others from committing such crimes. It was only ever used for them and the original gibbet rotted away, a second was struck by lightning and a third lasted nearly 100 years until it came down in a gale in 1949. The hill looked bare and unfamiliar without a gibbet so by popular request and public subscription a new one was erected with great ceremony in 1950.

Walk 4
MARSH BENHAM

Distance: 4 miles (6.4 km)

Map: OS Explorer 158 Newbury & Hungerford
Grid Ref: SU426675

How to get there: From the M4 take the A34 south then follow signs for the A4 towards Hungerford. After about 2 miles you will see a sign for Marsh Benham and indeed for The Red House itself to the left, follow signs to the pub. **Sat Nav:** RG20 8LY.

Parking: The pub has a good-sized car park, but please ask the landlord's permission to leave your car before setting off on the walk.

This walk follows the main track through Hamstead Park, a lovely park with a lake and rolling green hills. There is also a very pleasant bit of the Kennet and Avon Canal towpath to look forward to towards the end of the route. There are no stiles on this walk.

THE RED HOUSE is a traditional thatched pub, popular with locals. The British menu includes all the regular pub favourites, which can be washed down with local ales and

hand-picked wines. There is pleasant beer garden, bar area where dogs are welcome and more formal dining at the rear. There are separate A la Carte, lunch and Sunday lunch menus, all of which are full of enticing looking dishes at the usual sort of prices.
⊕ theredhousepub.com ☎ 01635 582017

The Walk

1 Turn left out of the pub car park, then at the road junction turn left again, signposted to **Hamstead Marshall**, in the direction of the railway. Cross over the level crossing and stay on the road passing **Marsh Benham House**, then crossing the bridges over the canal and the **River Kennet**. As the road starts to bear right turn left through a kissing gate into **Hamstead Park**.

2 At a junction of paths head straight, onto a concrete track. If you would like to take a detour to see the gate piers mentioned in the 'Places of Interest' turn right here instead and follow the path around to the right until they appear in front of you, then return to the junction of paths. There is a smaller path to the left

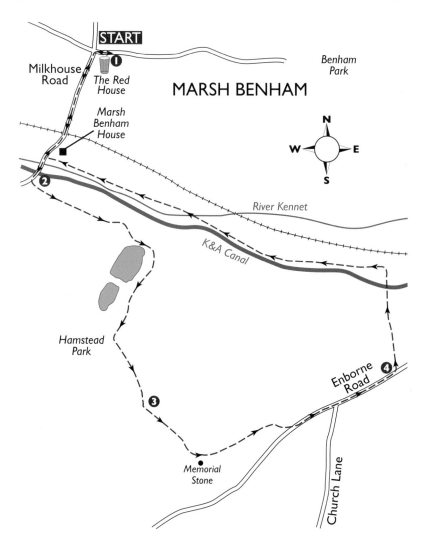

with nice views of the **River Kennet**, but the concrete track is your route. Stay on this path as it crosses a cattle grid and bends to the right around a lake. Follow the track up the hill and round to the left. Ignore the turning to the left, but as the track starts to bear right head straight on, down towards a gate. Go through the kissing gate and keep on in the same direction until you join the concrete path.

3 Turn left to rejoin the main track following a yellow footpath arrow. When you reach a junction of footpaths continue on the track as it bears left past an **American paratrooper memorial stone**. Stay on the track until you exit the park via two kissing gates. Turn left on the road following the yellow footpath sign. Walk on the road

for about 500 metres, passing a turning on the right, until a clear footpath sign points left – follow this onto a concrete track.

4 Keep going straight on as the track turns into a wide path and then through a kissing gate onto a smaller path. Walk past a metal gate and over the canal bridge, then turn left onto the **Kennet and Avon Canal** towpath. Stay on this very pleasant stretch of towpath for about a mile, passing a weir/sluice gate along the way, until you reach a bridge. Go through a gate onto the road and turn right to follow the road back to **The Red House**.

Places of Interest

Hamstead Marshall, just a few miles away, is a small village with a lot of history. In the 12th and 13th centuries it was home to Earl Marshal, the monarch's chief adviser and administrator. The 1st Earl of Craven (1608-1697) built a mansion here, originally intended as a home for Charles I's sister but she died before its construction and sadly it burnt down in 1718. The Grade I listed gate piers are all that's left of the original house. To see them on the walk you can take a detour at point 2. The Cravens later expanded a hunting lodge to live in instead, and this still stands, privately occupied, in the centre of Hamstead Park. The family still owned the property up to the 1980s when it was put up for auction.

Walk 5
BAGNOR

Distance: 2¾ miles (4.5 km)

Map: OS Explorer 158 Newbury & Hungerford
Grid Ref: SU453693

How to get there: Leave the M4 at junction 13 and head south on the A34 (signposted Winchester and Southampton) for a couple of miles then exit at a sign for A4 Newbury and Hungerford, turn left at the roundabout and then follow brown signs for 'The Watermill Theatre' until you see The Blackbird on your right. **Sat Nav:** RG20 8AQ.

Parking: The Blackbird has some parking at the front or you could park in The Watermill Theatre's car park if there is space. Please remember to ask permission.

Although a fairly short walk, the route is packed with interest. You start in the pretty little village of Bagnor, with the excellent Watermill Theatre just round the corner (which also has a delightful restaurant), then head up a lovely tree-lined path to Snelsmore Common. The return journey passes a golf course and Donnington Castle before heading back to the pub. And if that's not enough to entice any kids you might have, there are two places along the way that sometimes have rope swings hanging from trees.

THE PUB THE BLACKBIRD is a family-run pub with a Michelin star restaurant in the heart of Bagnor village. It is family friendly, with a small kids' playground in the beer garden and a children's menu. The food is gastro pub fare and there is a set menu on Wednesday to Friday lunchtimes (they are closed Mondays and Tuesdays). The staff are friendly and the beer is good.
⊕ theblackbird.co.uk ☎ 01635 40005

The Walk

1 Turn right out of the pub and walk for 100 metres, with the houses on your right, until, above a 30 limit sign, you should see a public footpath sign. Turn right here, along a grassy drive, up to a kissing gate next to a wooden gate. Go through the gate and up the grassy slope (with a nice view behind you) to pass a

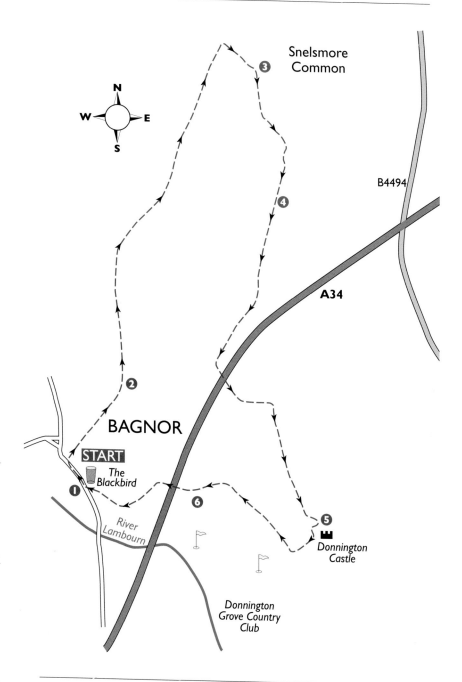

wooden bench into a gap in the trees, through a kissing gate and turn left on the byway.

2 Follow this lovely tree-lined path for about ½ mile then go straight on past a footpath on the right and one to the left, past a couple of cottages and up to a gate into **Snelsmore Common**. The path immediately forks here – take the left fork and follow alongside a fence on your left until that fence turns away left at which point you turn right, up the hill, to a big junction of paths with a little wooden bench.

3 Follow the purple dragonfly trail down the hill and over a platform next to a marshy area where you can look out for dragonflies, then up the steps on the other side. Keep following the dragonfly arrows rightish, along and then left to a wooded area where there are usually rope swings. Keep straight on until you reach a gate with paths heading in various directions. Go through the gate, out of the common, and past **Beau House** along a wide track.

4 Go past a footpath heading right, passing **Donnington Valley Golf Course** on your right. Stay on the bridleway as it turns into a concrete path that eventually bends left to cross a bridge over the A34. Stay on the path as it bends left up a brief hill, and then turn right on a bridleway, where you should get your first view of **Donnington Castle**. Stay on this track until you reach a metal gate. Go through the gate and as the path bears left you should see a gate on the right taking you into the castle grounds.

5 You will probably want to linger and have a good look around what is left of the twin-towered gatehouse and earthworks. When you're ready to carry on, the path is on the far side of the ruins to where you came in, going down the hill past a tree (not towards the car park) and round to the right. Go through a gate to join another path through the trees and down to where there is sometimes a rope swing. This path ends at a concrete path, bear slightly left onto another tree-lined path parallel to the golf course.

6 When you emerge onto a concrete track turn right and follow signs for the 2nd tee, and a footpath sign, crossing another bridge over the A34. At the end of the bridge turn left on a public footpath and follow the path down the hill to a kissing gate next to a large wooden gate. Go through it and turn half right onto a gravel drive, between houses, that takes you back to The Blackbird.

Places of Interest

Donnington Castle is a ruined medieval castle. It was founded by Sir Richard Abberbury the Elder in 1386 and was bought by Thomas Chaucer, son of poet Geoffrey Chaucer, before the castle was taken under royal control during the Tudor period. During the First English Civil War the castle was held by the royalist Sir John Boys and withstood an 18-month siege; after the garrison eventually surrendered, Parliament voted to demolish Donnington Castle in 1646. Only the original gatehouse survives.

During the Second World War **Snelsmore Common** was taken over for military use, and had large quantities of petrol stored in jerrycans by the 3900 Quartermaster Gasoline Supply Company stockpiled for the Normandy landings. During 1995-6 woodland at the south end of the common became an early base for campaigners protesting against the proposed Newbury bypass. Following the eviction of the protesters, the construction of the road went ahead through part of the common, and an equivalent area of common was added to the west.

Walk 6
CROOKHAM

Distance: 4 miles (6.4 km)

Map: OS Explorer 158 Newbury & Hungerford
Grid Ref: SU537643

How to get there: Take the A4 towards Thatcham (between Theale and Newbury). Crookham is signposted from one of the roundabouts (at the east end of Thatcham). Signs should lead you over a railway crossing, past the common and along to the pub, which you can't miss from the road. **Sat Nav:** RG19 8EA.

Parking: The pub has a good sized car park. Note that parking is reserved for customers, but the food is great so we recommend you factor in a stop here, just let the landlord know when you leave your car that you'll be visiting the pub on your return.

The real charm of this walk lies in the unexpected variety it offers. What feels like a secret entrance to a public footpath whisks you quickly away from the road, and down into glorious Berkshire farmland. Here you'll make your way alongside open fields, through woodland, along a winding riverside (keep an eye out for kingfishers here) and onto the end of Crookham Common at the eastern end of Greenham Common.

THE PUB THE TRAVELLERS FRIEND is a traditional family-friendly pub. They serve a range of light bites, as well as classic pub grub for the heartier appetite. There is also a carvery on Sunday. The beer garden (plus playground area for the kids) is perfect for warmer days. An added bonus is the village shop to the side, which sells local produce, including homemade pies and cakes.

⊕ thetravellersfriend.co.uk ☎ 0118 971 3156

The Walk

❶ From the pub car park turn right onto the verge of the main road. After about 50 metres you will see a public footpath sign pointing to the left, follow this along the middle of three tracks past a gate with a yellow footpath arrow onto a track. Keep left past a house, through a small bit of tree-lined path then along the right edge of a field, gradually down the hill and into copse bearing slightly right.

❷ As you reach a cottage turn right in front of it and follow the path across a small bridge, then bear slightly left across the middle of a field to another wooden bridge. Go through a gate and head across the next field in the same direction towards a post with a footpath arrow. Head left through an open gate and alongside the **River Enborne** until you reach a wooden bridge with footpath signs.

❸ Cross the bridge and turn immediately right onto the riverside path. Go through the kissing gate and stay on the winding riverside path for about a mile until you pass through another kissing gate and onto a lane. Turn right and then fork left, where the road fords across the river. Cross a metal bridge over the river and then rejoin the road. Head uphill and past a metal gate to the main road.

❹ Turn right on the edge of the road for just about 20 metres then cross over the road with care to take the narrow path into

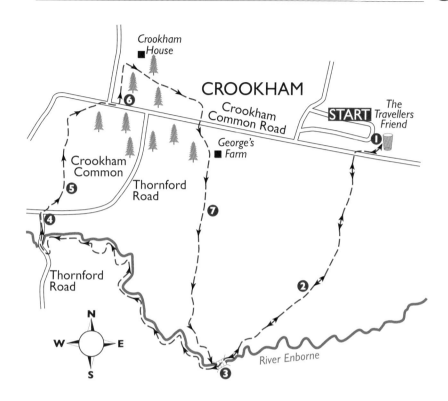

Crookham Common. Follow this path as it turns immediately right (the path resembles a stream bed at this point), up the hill, then left and keep going in the same direction as you reach the top of the hill. When you pass a tree with blue rope hanging from it turn left onto a narrow footpath.

5 Keep on this path as another path joins from the right, following a sign with a black butterfly in a purple arrow. Keep following the black butterfly through several junctions of paths until you reach a small car park (which has an information board about the common). Head for the far end of the car park where a small path leads you along to a track, turn left on the track and carefully cross the main road to another track opposite.

6 Follow the track up to a property and turn right onto an unmarked path into the woods, passing **Crookham House** on your left and a reservoir on your right. Cross over a tarmac path and carry straight on into further woods. When you emerge onto a concrete track turn right up to the main road. Cross with care and proceed on the track opposite as it bears left then right past **George's Farm** and past a green gate.

7 Dog-leg slightly left, when prompted to do so, and proceed along the right edge of a field down to an open gate. Bear half-left across the field, following white-topped posts, back to the wooden bridge you crossed about an hour ago. Bear left here along the riverside path and retrace your steps back to **The Travellers Friend**.

Places of Interest

Greenham Common is a name that will be very familiar to anyone who lived in this country in the 1980s, but it had actually been used for military purposes long before then. The first record is from the First Battle of Newbury, in 1643, one of the battles of the English Civil War. The large open spaces of the commons have been used many times since as army camps, then, in 1942, the RAF turned it into an airfield, which was given over to the USAAF the following year for their operations. The US continued to use the site after the Second World War and even before the 1980s protests were never far away. However, it was in the 1980s and 90s that the protests became much more strident, well-supported and widely publicised and this was because of the decision in 1980 to stand nuclear-armed cruise missiles at Greenham Common.

In 1992 the USAAF handed command back to the RAF, then in 1997 the Greenham Common Trust bought the airbase selling the open land to the Council. More recently the common has appeared as the fictional planet D'Qar in episodes 7 and 8 of the main Star Wars series.

Walk 7
MORTIMER

Distance: 3¾ miles (6 km)

Map: OS Explorer 159 Reading, Wokingham & Pangbourne
Grid Ref: SU655645

How to get there: From the M4 leave at Junction 11 and take the A33 towards Basingstoke. After about a mile take a right turn towards Mereoak Lane, then at the roundabout turn left and keep following this road until you arrive in Mortimer. The Horse and Groom is on the left and a public car park on the right. **Sat Nav:** RG7 3RD.

Parking: Park in the public car park opposite the Horse and Groom.

Starting and finishing at a village cricket green, and taking in woodland paths, pretty ponds, open fields and a super-friendly local pub, this route ticks off just about everything you'd want in a classic pub walk. The village of Mortimer, just a few miles south of the M4, doesn't get the press that many others in Berkshire do, but it's well worth the detour for this lovely country walk.

THE PUB THE HORSE AND GROOM has a decent sized beer garden to the side of the pub, the staff are friendly and the food is reasonably priced. There is also a good playground near the car park.

🌐 No website ☎ 0118 933 2813

However, if you're looking for something a little different then you could head about a mile down the road to **THE TURNERS ARMS**, which has a full Thai menu as well as the usual English pub food. There is a good-sized garden and a welcoming open fire for the colder days. To get there, turn right out of car park then left after the church and keep going until you see the pub on your right.

🌐 theturnersarms.co.uk ☎ 0118 933 2961

The Walk

1 From the public car park, head away from the pub and towards the right of the cricket pavilion. Bear slightly right across the cricket pitch towards a metal kissing gate which is slightly obscured by a small tree. Go through the gate and along a path to a field. Keep going in the same direction towards the far right corner of the field where you will find another kissing gate. Go through the gate, cross the road and go through another kissing gate into some woods. Keep on the main path as another path joins from the right and follow the yellow arrow to the edge of the woods.

2 When you emerge into a field there are footpaths going straight on or right, go straight on across the field, through a kissing

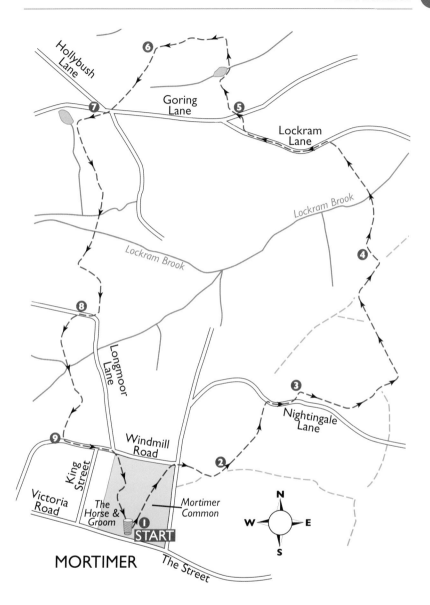

gate and along a path at the left edge of the field to another
gate and onto a small road. Turn right on the road, following
the recreational route sign, for about 100 metres until you see
a public footpath sign pointing left through a small gap. Take

the path down and over a couple of small bridges to the edge of another field and turn right.

3 Follow the right edge of the field and when you see a footpath heading right through a gap in the hedgerow keep going straight on until, shortly after, you go through a gap in the hedge and turn left following a footpath sign. Follow the left edge of the field along to a junction of paths and then turn right to stay on the left edge of the same field. After less than 100 metres there is a gap in the hedge on your left. Go through the gap and follow the path on the right edge of this field.

4 The path soon winds its way into another field where a footpath sign will point you to the right. Follow this path over a wooden bridge, straight on across the next field, then past a large log and onto a small lane. Turn left following the recreational route sign. Follow this lane around to the right, past some cottages on the right and then just after you pass **Lockram Cottage** on your left take an unmarked path on the right along to the main road.

5 Carefully cross the main road to the sign for **Wokefield Common** and follow the main track that curls slightly to the right. Head down to where the path skirts around a lovely pond. At a junction of paths head left following a blue arrow passing another pond to the left, a footpath heading right and a **BMX track** on the left, to another path junction where you go straight on following the recreational route sign.

6 When you come to a junction with a bridleway follow the bridleway

forking to the left and keep going straight on past a post with lots of arrows, past another pond and straight on across another path. The path is less clear here, but try to keep in a straight line heading towards the sound of the road ahead and you should arrive at the road next to a crossroads. Cross over the road and follow the unmarked path which bears right towards a car park.

7 Head straight across the car park to the back left corner, where there is an information board. At the junction of paths turn left following the recreational route sign. Keep going straight on along this path until you emerge near a house, go straight on along the path between fences to the left of the house. Follow this path down the hill, over a stream, and up the other side. At a T-junction take the public footpath to the left. Shortly take a small unmarked path on the right and it will lead you to a road.

8 Cross the road and head towards the house opposite where you will see a path heading off to the right. Follow this path as it bears left between two hedges, then after climbing a small hill you will emerge at a junction with a byway sign pointing right. Turn right, then left, to skirt the tree, then right again on the slightly bigger of the two paths. Ignore the small path heading left and then turn left onto a larger path. At a junction with footpath signs turn left and follow this path around to the right and between houses down to a road.

9 Turn left on the pavement. Carry on past **King Street** on your right and then, after you pass **Longmoor Lane** on your left, cross over and go through a kissing gate. Turn right across a field to head towards a large gate with a gap next to it. Go through the gap and along to another gap next to the playground. From here you can see the pub and the car park.

Places of Interest

The village of **Silchester**, a couple of miles south of Mortimer (into Hampshire), is well-known as an archaeological site and is where the Roman town of Calleva Atrebatum once stood. The walls and amphitheatre are unusually well preserved as the area has never been built over. There is a car park and you can visit for free.

Walk 8
WOOLHAMPTON

Distance: 5 miles (8 km)

Map: OS Explorer 159 Reading, Wokingham & Pangbourne
Grid Ref: SU572664

How to get there: Woolhampton is on the A4 between Thatcham and Theale. From the M4, leave at junction 12 and take the A4 towards Thatcham and Newbury. After about 6 miles you will come to Woolhampton, turn left opposite The Angel pub (signposted for the station) and cross over the railway and the river to reach The Rowbarge. **Sat Nav:** RG7 5SH.

Parking: The Rowbarge has a decent-sized car park at the rear, but please ask the landlord's permission before leaving your car.

The Rowbarge pub, with its expansive beer garden right on the banks of the River Kennet, is the start and finish point for this walk, and it certainly takes some beating. The early section of the route takes in a lovely stretch of river, while the subsequent stages, along bridleways and through wooded paths, are equally idyllic.

At the halfway point, in the sleepy little village of Beenham, there's another opportunity for sustenance, at the excellent Six Bells.

THE PUB **THE ROWBARGE** is a lovely characterful pub right on the banks of the River Kennet. Originally listed as a beer shop called William IV (when William IV was King), it became The Rowbarge in the late 1850s. It has had many interesting landlords over the years including former actor Laurence (Larry) Naismith who appeared in many well known films of the 1950-70s. The food is delicious with a broad range of dishes to suit different tastes and requirements, plus roasts on a Sunday.
⊕ www.brunningandprice.co.uk/rowbarge ☎ 0118 971 2213

THE SIX BELLS is an award-winning cosy country pub, with equally delightful food. It has also been in *CAMRA's Good Beer Guide* for the last 10 years.
⊕ thesixbells.co.uk ☎ 0118 971 3368

The Walk

❶ From **The Rowbarge** head towards the swing bridge and turn right before you reach it, onto the towpath. After about ½ mile cross over the footbridge and continue along the other side of the

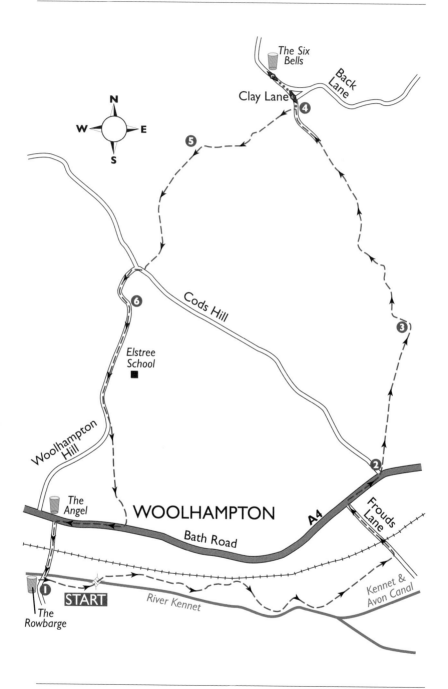

river until you reach a gate. Go through the gate and up to the road. Turn left over the railway bridge and along to the main road (A4). Turn right onto the pavement and cross at the crossing, then continue on the pavement on the other side of the road.

2 After about 150 metres there is a turning to the left signposted to **Upper Woolhampton**. When you cross this road you should see a public bridleway sign pointing to a metal gate. Go through this gate and cross a field, in the same direction, heading for the large gap in the hedges where you will see a blue footpath arrow guiding you towards the corner of the woods. Exit the field through an open gate and continue on the path with the woods to your left.

3 At the end of this path you should see a wooden post with various arrows, take the left byway. Soon you will reach a junction with a footpath heading left; head right on the byway though and when you reach another junction with a bridleway head left. Ignore the footpath on the right and continue uphill on the byway until the track turns into a road. Ignore another footpath heading right and shortly after that you will see a footpath sign pointing left.

4 If you would like to visit **The Six Bells** pub go straight along this road, bearing leftish on **Clay Lane** for about 100 metres and at the end you will see this lovely looking pub. To continue the walk turn left on the narrow footpath to pass through a kissing gate, and then along into some woods. Where the path forks, take the right fork. At the end of the woods you will come to a 5-way junction of paths, take the 2nd left, which is a bridleway heading diagonally across a field.

5 Cross the field and continue on a path into copse, following the blue arrow. When you come to a road in a housing estate, cross straight over and continue on the path opposite as it bends slightly right. When you emerge onto a road look right and you can see **Douai School**, now redeveloped as private housing, (and Abbey if you continue past the school), but to continue, cross the road and enter the sports grounds, then immediately turn right and follow the path around the tennis courts and along to where it ends at a road.

6 Turn left onto the pavement and pass **Woolhampton Primary School**, the church and **Elstree School**. When the road starts to bear right, go straight on following the public footpath sign onto a path between the hedge and cricket pitch. Follow this narrow path down the hill then bear slightly left to reach a field. Follow the right edge of the field down towards the main road, until you emerge into a garage. Turn right onto the pavement of the A4 and carefully cross over when possible. Turn left opposite **The Angel** pub (also very nice) and head across the railway and swing bridge back to **The Rowbarge**.

Places of Interest

Douai Abbey is a Benedictine monastery that originated in 1903 when the Benedictine community of St Edmund was expelled from Douai in France, and the site was offered to them by the Bishop of Portsmouth. They combined their school, St Edmund's College, with St Mary's College to form Douai School, which was a public school until 1999 when it closed. ⊕ douaiabbey.org.uk

Walk 9
UPPER BUCKLEBURY

Distance: 4 miles (6.4 km)

Map: OS Explorer 158 Newbury & Hungerford
Grid Ref: SU542685

How to get there: Take the A4 towards Thatcham and Upper Bucklebury is signposted from one of the roundabouts (at the east end of Thatcham). Keep following signs for Upper Bucklebury and The Cottage Inn is on the main road through the village on the left. **Sat Nav:** RG7 6QJ.

Parking: The pub has quite a large car park for patrons, alternatively there is roadside parking along the main street.

This fine walk is largely through Bucklebury Common, one of the largest commons in the South of England, covering 860 acres. Be sure to follow the directions carefully as there are lots of footpaths. You will pass through lower Bucklebury, home to the Middleton family, and walk straight through the middle of Bucklebury Farm Park (see Places of Interest for more information). Then it's back along some peaceful paths to the award-winning Cottage Inn.

THE PUB THE COTTAGE INN has won the Best Community Pub award four times in recent years and it's not hard to see why. There is an outside patio area, an animal enclosure, a paddock with children's play equipment and the open fire offers a warm welcome in the colder months. The staff are also very friendly and helpful. The menu descriptions sound appetising, and include a children's menu, lunch menu of sandwiches and jacket potatoes as well as a main menu catering for larger appetites. All are reasonably priced and the reviews are good.

⊕ thecottageinnupperbucklebury.co.uk ☎ 01635 864544

The Walk _____

❶ From **The Cottage Inn** car park turn left onto the pavement, ignoring the first footpath sign on the left, and walk about 300 metres, past **Bucklebury Memorial Hall**, until you see a byway arrow pointing left and a public bridleway sign pointing right slightly further along the road. Take the bridleway into the common and go straight on over a small road and then a

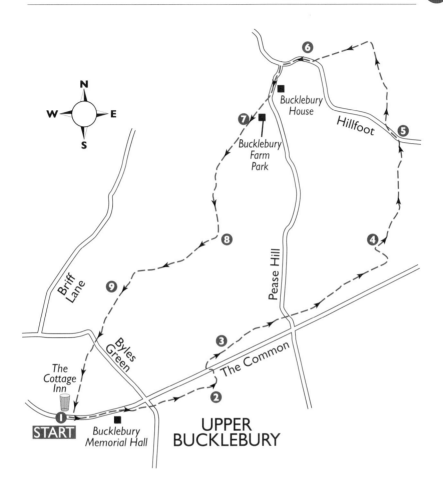

concrete track. Keep straight on at the junction of paths. When you emerge onto copse take the left path when it forks, across towards a small hill.

❷ Go up the mound and at the top bear half left down the other side. Turn left here and follow the indistinct path towards the road (the correct path goes a few metres right of a large puddle, but if you miss that just aim for a bridle path sign you should be able to see on the road). Cross over the road and turn left briefly then right following a restricted byway sign. Almost immediately you'll come to a junction of byways, turn right following a red arrow.

3 At the next junction, go straight on following a red arrow again. You may need to use side paths as, in places, puddles often cover the whole path if the weather has been wet. Ignore the bridleway heading off left, cross over a small road and carry straight on past another junction of byways. After about 200 metres look out for a path on the left, next to a footpath post with a blue arrow. Follow this onto a smaller path for about 100 metres, then turn right on the path that crosses left to right.

4 Follow this clear and well-used path along to another post with a blue arrow. Follow it to the left keeping a fence to your right. As you pass a house on the right there is a fallen footpath post at a junction, carry straight on to where the path appears to fork, but the right-hand path is just to avoid a particularly muddy patch. The path forks again just before another post, take the right fork to avoid the stream that crosses the path. Carry on along the path until you emerge onto a track next to a road.

5 Turn left on the road and soon you will see a sign saying **Brownsgate** on the right and a footpath on the left, but the footpath you want is a few metres past Brownsgate on the right. Go over a stile and head across a field to the far corner, where it winds down to another stile. Cross the stile and head straight across the next field towards a footpath junction in the middle of the fields. Cross the little bridge and turn left towards a house. Go through a stile next to a large metal gate and then turn right on the road.

6 Follow the road round to the left and turn left at the road junction. Head up the road for about 100 metres until you come to **Bucklebury Farm Park** on your right, **Bucklebury House** on your left and a footpath just along on the right. Take the footpath through a tall kissing gate into a field and bear half-left across the field towards the main car park and another tall kissing gate. Go through the car park and along the drive up to the farm, following a couple of yellow footpath arrows.

7 Carry straight on through a gate into the first field, then up to two large gates next to each other. Go through the left gate, and up to the far corner of the field to cross a stile with a yellow arrow. You can avoid these fields by turning left after the farm building and then right up the grassy path to this point. Cross over another stile with a footpath arrow and proceed next to a fence along to a tall kissing gate. Go through the gate and head left on the broad path.

8 After about 100 metres you will come to a junction with a bridleway to the left and a footpath to the right, turn right onto the path into the woods. This fairly clear path takes you down, then up, and then down again until you join up with a larger path, turn right on this path. Ignore two footpaths heading right and one byway heading left, and then go straight along the road for about 50 metres until you see a byway heading left. Take this byway.

9 Go straight on past a byway heading right along to a road. Turn right briefly, then left following a footpath sign, past a row of houses to a kissing gate. Go through the gate and bear leftish across the field, through an open gate and straight along the left edge of the next field and through another kissing gate. Bear right, passing the rear of the pub's play area, and follow the path down to the main road where you turn right back to **The Cottage Inn**.

Places of Interest

Bucklebury Farm Park is a great place to visit with children of all ages. There are plenty of farm animals for them to pat and larger animals include llamas, lambs and peacocks. There's also a tractor safari to see and feed the deer herd, plus an adventure playground and jumping pillow. ⊕ buckleburyfarmpark.co.uk

Walk 10

FRILSHAM

Distance: 4 miles (6.4 km)

Map: OS Explorer 158 Newbury & Hungerford
Grid Ref: SU553731

How to get there: Drive to Hermitage either on the B4009 from Newbury, or north on the A34 from J13 of the M4 then immediately right. From Hermitage the road to Yattendon is clearly signposted. When you reach Yattendon turn right, where you should see a brown sign for the Pot Kiln. Follow the road over the motorway and then shortly along to the pub, preceded by a car park. **Sat Nav:** RG18 0XX.

Parking: Either park in the public car park next to the pub or in the pub's own car park towards the rear.

This walk takes in some lovely woodland and is particularly nice in spring when the bluebells are out. The walk is pretty flat with no stiles, but like any woodland walk certain parts can get quite muddy so choose footwear accordingly.

THE PUB THE POT KILN'S location is pretty secluded, with no other buildings in sight and plenty of footpaths heading off in various directions. The food is very much centred on game and local produce and options for a vegetarian are pretty limited, but if you want a meaty treat in a stunning location then this is the pub for you. Whenever one of the broadsheets does a roundup of the best country pubs the Pot Kiln is usually on the list, and it's not hard to see why.

⊕ potkiln.org ☎ 01635 201366

The Walk

❶ From the front of the **Pot Kiln** car park various footpaths are signed, follow the **'Recreational Route'** sign heading left along the road. After about 50 metres there is a public footpath sign pointing right, follow that through a gate, along the left edge of a field, through another gate, over a small bridge and along the left edge of the next field. Go through another gate and continue in the same direction on a path into some woods.

❷ Cross straight over a track and into deeper woods. At a junction of byways, carry straight on. Continue through some quite muddy patches (if the weather has been wet) and past a **Recreational Route** arrow. When you reach another post, follow the arrows pointing left onto a smaller path. Follow this lovely path through more muddy bits (you may also have to duck under some overgrown brambles), through two kissing gates and then left onto a gravel drive down to a small road.

❸ Cross the road and go straight on along a path into copse down to a point where it looks like you'll have to wade across the **River Pang**. Bear left just before the river, not crossing over the

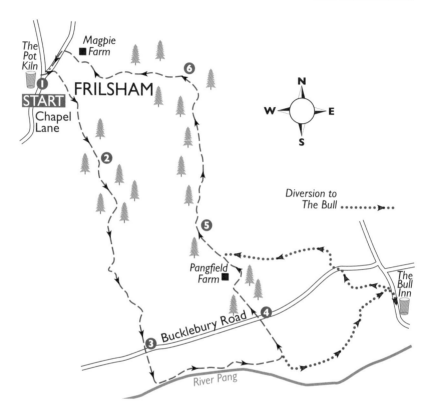

little bridge. Follow this riverside path through a metal gate and eventually another gate onto a broad track passing left to right. Turn left up to a small road.

4 Carefully cross over the road, following the byway sign up another driveway. At the top of the driveway the purple arrow points straight on, but this path is partially blocked, so follow the signs saying '**Preferred Path**' to the right and then left between the farm buildings until you see a crossroads of footpaths ahead. Go straight on, alongside the line of trees to the left and then rejoin the main path by bearing left at a gap next to a gate and turning right onto a path between trees.

5 Carry on through the woods until you reach a junction. Going left would be a short cut that would take you back to the byway junction in point 2. Otherwise, go straight on, ignoring the footpath through a gate on the right. After a while a smaller path forks right off the larger track and leads to a metal gate. Go through the gate and follow the arrow across a field to a bridleway signpost on the other side. Turn left at the signpost along the edge of the woods and then bear slightly left on an indistinct path across a field towards a wooden gate.

6 Turn left, following the yellow arrow (rather than going through the gate) along the right edge of the field to a metal kissing gate. Go through the gate then straight on across the field towards a wooden footpath post. Pass this post and another one with footpath arrows, turn right at another footpath sign and then straight on at a junction with a bridleway towards a farm and past a **Christmas tree nursery**. Turn left along **Magpie Farm's** drive and along to a road. Turn left on the road and after 100 metres you will see the first footpath you took, and after another 50 metres you will arrive back at the pub.

Places of Interest

The Living Rainforest in the village of Hampstead Norreys is less than a ten-minute drive away. Here you will find an indoor tropical rainforest, ecological and educational centre with over 700 species of exotic plants and animals. ⊕ livingrainforest.org

Walk 11

UPPER BASILDON

Distance: 3½ miles (5.5 km)

Map: OS Explorer 159 Reading, Wokingham & Pangbourne
Grid Ref: SU597761

How to get there: From the east follow signs for Pangbourne (from junction 12 of the M4) then when you pass through Tidmarsh follow signs for Upper Basildon (left). Turn left as you enter the village and you will soon see the pub on your right. From the west drive to Hermitage either on the B4009 from Newbury, or north on the A34 from J13 of the M4 then immediately right. From Hermitage follow signs for Yattendon then carry on and ignore the first sign for Upper Basildon, but shortly afterwards turn left towards Pangbourne then take the next left, signposted Upper Basildon, and you come straight to the pub. **Sat Nav:** RG8 8NG.

Parking: The Red Lion has a decent-sized car park, but please ask the landlord's permission before leaving your car.

This lovely walk is quite short and mostly flat so should be suitable for all. The paths are mainly tree-lined so good for a drizzly day or a very hot day when you might want a bit of shade. In late summer this would be a good walk for blackberry picking.

THE PUB THE RED LION is a traditional country pub with oak beams, a warm atmosphere and a large beer garden to the rear. The gastropub-style food is good, with a decent selection of starters, mains and sandwiches (not on Sundays though) at fairly reasonable prices, plus the usual selection of roasts on a Sunday.

🌐 theredlionupperbasildon.co.uk ☎ 01491 671234

The Walk

1 From **The Red Lion** car park cross the main road and head away from the pub on the **Yattendon Road** for about 400 metres until, where the road bends, you will see footpath signs on both sides of the road. Take the footpath, which is the 2nd turning on the right. Follow the path through a short section of woods, then straight on across a field, through a rickety metal kissing gate,

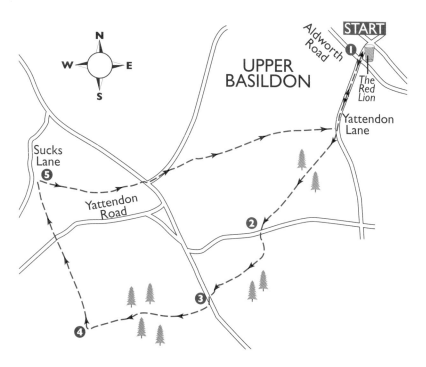

and straight on across the next field (the path may not be obvious here) towards the far left corner. There should be a stile here and you can see where there once was one, but it's still pretty simple to cross over the low section of fence.

2 Turn left to the road. Cross over the road carefully, then follow the gravel byway opposite and at the T-junction turn right. Shortly, this track passes a closed gate on your left and the footpath branches off to the left into the woods (the footpath sign has been uprooted). Follow this path alongside the fence and through what probably used to be a gate, then down through the woods onto a driveway between houses and along to a road.

3 Cross the road carefully and take the lane opposite, signposted **Mapletons**, and after about 200 metres, just after a large metal gate, a footpath heads straight on where the road bends, take this path. At the time of writing this path was a bit overgrown with nettles, so take care. Soon this turns into a lovely tree-lined path.

4 When you reach a junction with a bridleway turn right to head straight across a field and into **Ashampstead Common** opposite. You will then pass three crossroads with other bridleways, each time head straight on following the bridleway marked 7. You will also need to cross a road between the  2nd and 3rd junction. When you reach the edge of the common, with a house ahead and left of you, take the path that almost doubles back on yourself to the right.

5 Follow the main path along the left edge of the common until you come to a road, cross over and take the road opposite, signposted **Upper Basildon**, for less than 100 metres until you see a byway sign forking off to the right. Follow this path up a slightly unexpected hill, then continue as it flattens out into another pleasant tree-lined path and continue until you reach the road you started on. Turn left and head back to the pub.

Places of Interest

Basildon Park is well worth a visit. The house was built between 1776 and 1783 for Sir Francis Sykes who made his fortune working for the British East India Company. It was designed by John Carr in the Palladian style but was never fully completed. The house passed through a succession of owners but by 1910 was standing empty. In 1914, it was requisitioned by the British Government as an army convalescent hospital. During the Second World War, the house was again requisitioned and served as a barracks, a training ground for tanks, and finally a prisoner of war camp. The house was later lovingly completely restored and refurnished by the second Lord Iliffe and his wife (though the demise of the house in the early 20th century was mainly due to the first Lord Iliffe!) and then handed over to the National Trust in 1978.
⊕ nationaltrust.org.uk/basildon-park.

Walk 12
PANGBOURNE

Distance: 3 miles (5 km)

Map: OS Explorer 159 Reading, Wokingham & Pangbourne
Grid Ref: SU632767

How to get there: Pangbourne is well signposted from junction 12 of the M4 and surrounding areas. Follow signs towards Beale Park and Basildon Park and you will see The Swan on the right, opposite the railway station. **Sat Nav:** RG8 7DU.

Parking: The pub only has a small car park, so use the public railway car park opposite if necessary.

Quite short, completely flat, and easy to follow, this walk should suit everyone. It also features a lovely stretch of the Thames Path. What more could you want from a walk? Oh yes a riverside pub waiting for you at the finish, it's got that as well. There's a good spot for feeding the ducks/geese/swans early on too.

THE PUB THE SWAN is a beautiful 17th-century listed building with oak beams and open fires in the winter. However, the biggest draw has to be the fine terrace overlooking the River Thames. It's actually surprisingly difficult to find good riverside pubs in Berkshire so The Swan is a real treat. For early birds there is an enticing brunch menu but the gastropub-style seasonal lunch menu looks very nice too. It's probably worth booking a table, especially if you want to sit on the terrace, as it's a popular spot. ⊕ swanpangbourne.co.uk ☎ 0118 984 4494

The Walk

❶ Turn left out of **The Swan** and before you reach the railway bridge turn left onto **The Wharf** (if you look carefully you can see a public footpath sign) and take the narrow path left of the railing. Turn left at the end of this path. Head straight on over a track and along to a road, cross over the road and turn left onto a pavement until the pavement ends at a footpath sign showing the **Thames Path** going leftish and straight on. Go through a gap in the hedge and turn left through the car park of the **Dolphin Centre** to a kissing gate in the left corner.

❷ Go through the gate and onto the path by the **River Thames** (past a duck feeding area) and continue on the path through copse and over a small bridge. Keep going until you cross a bit of raised path over some reed beds. Walk over a bridge and through

a gate where you turn right, heading away from the **Thames**. Stay on this path with a fence to your left and a little stream on the right until you reach a large gate. Pass by the gate and turn left to pass through the railway arch and follow the track around to the right, where shortly, you will see a footpath sign pointing through a gate on the left.

3 Follow the path along the right edge of a field until you reach a road. Turn right onto the pavement and cross over when convenient, passing a school on your left. Turn left onto **Kennedy Drive**. Stay on this road as it passes the back of the school then, as it bears around to the right, look out on the left for a large telegraph pole after which an unmarked pathway heads left. Follow the path to a gate with a yellow footpath arrow on it. Go through this gate and a kissing gate and bear right along the right edge of a field.

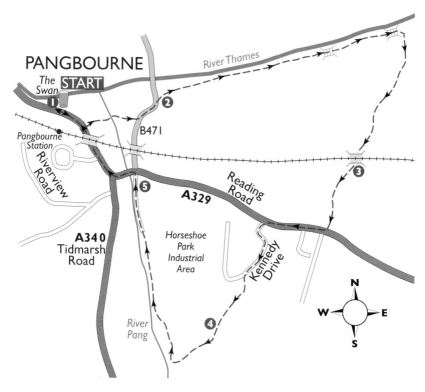

4 Soon you will see a kissing gate to the right with various footpath signs, but just carry on in the same direction until you reach an open gate. Go through the gate and then straight on across the field until you reach the **River Pang**. Turn right before the river and pass to the left of a clump of trees to a metal kissing gate. Go through onto a clear path between trees and keep straight on as it turns into a cul-de-sac.

5 At the end of the road turn left to pass the **Co-op**, then cross over at the zebra crossing and continue along to the roundabout. Turn right towards the railway bridge. You'll need to cross the road to go under the bridge, then cross back again and proceed past the road that leads to **Pangbourne station** and along to **The Swan**.

Places of Interest

Beale Park is a wildlife park and gardens situated between the villages of Pangbourne and Lower Basildon. Highlights include the collection of small exotic animals, farm animals and birds, children's play areas and paddling pool, and the miniature train which tours the park. ⊕ bealepark.org.uk

Walk 13
READING

Distance: 2¾ miles (4.3 km)

Map: OS Explorer 159 Reading, Wokingham & Pangbourne
Grid Ref: SU725735

How to get there: From junction 11 of the M4 take the A33 towards Reading. Turn right onto the A329, then after about ½ mile turn left onto Watlington Street and follow the road round to the right onto King's Road. Turn left onto Orts Road and the pub is on the left down Canal Way. **Sat Nav:** RG1 3HJ (pub) or RG1 4PX (Queen's Road car park).

Parking: The pub has small car park or the nearest NCP is the Queen's Road car park.

This short walk is packed with local history as well as lovely scenery along the canal and riverside paths. Despite never really leaving Reading's bustling town centre there are meadows, public gardens, some lovely river views and the abbey ruins to explore.

THE PUB THE FISHERMAN'S COTTAGE is pretty popular in the area, but if you're visiting from further afield you'd be unlikely to stumble upon it by chance, which is a shame because it's a little gem of a pub. The main pub building is tiny, but a large conservatory has been added to the side for diners, plus there are tables outside at the front next to the canal, and a lovely

terrace at the rear with little huts, like booths, along the back that you can sit in. They're in *CAMRA's Good Beer Guide* for their ales and the food is good.

🌐 thefishermanscottagereading.co.uk

☎ 0118 956 0432

The Walk

1 *From the Queen's Road car park* turn right and walk along **Queen's Road**. Keep right to stay on **Queen's Road** until you reach the junction with **King's Road**. Turn left and at the bridge turn right down some steps to the towpath. Keep walking on the towpath and you will soon arrive at the **Fisherman's Cottage**.

1 *From the front of the pub,* turn right on the canal towpath, immediately passing **Blake's Lock**. Continue past another pub, under a pedestrian bridge and then under two railway bridges and now, with the **Thames** in front of you use the **Horseshoe Bridge** behind you to cross over the **Kennet**. As you exit the bridge continue straight onto the **Thames Path**. There are lovely views of the river on the right.

2 Continue on the path, past a supermarket entrance, then go straight on across **King's Meadow** when the path parts company with the **Thames** briefly (with a view of **The Blade** tower to your left). The path rejoins the **Thames** at **Caversham Lock**. Cross over the lock and look for a small path to your left that looks a bit like a dead end. Go down this path and turn left. Cross over the Thames on the weir bridge then continue on the path on the far side.

3 After about 100 metres you will see a turning on the right with a sign for **View Island**. *View Island was a derelict boatyard which Reading Borough Council bought and restored in 1998, it's now a lovely spot for a stroll or a picnic, with several benches overlooking the Thames.* To explore this 4-acre wildlife haven follow this wooden pathway to a junction with a path, where you can turn either way to do a circuit around this pretty island, then come back up the wooden path to where you started and turn right. If you don't

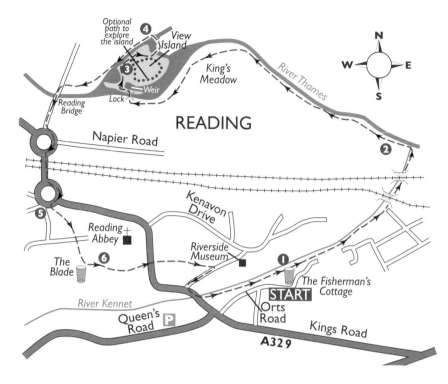

wish to do this bit just carry straight on and you will come to a small wooden bridge, cross this and turn left onto a concrete path next to the river, through **Hill's Meadow**.

4 This path takes you back to the **Thames**. You need to fork right at a junction in the path to get to, and cross over, **Reading Bridge**. Follow the road to a large roundabout, where you'll need to bear left to a crossing in order to go straight on under the railway bridge and along to another roundabout. Turn left to reach a crossing and at the other side turn right onto the pavement for about 30 metres until you see an entrance to **Forbury Gardens** on your left.

5 Enter the gardens and head straight for the lion statue in the middle, which was erected to commemorate the 19th-century Afghan campaigns. Walk between the lion and the bandstand to exit the gardens opposite the abbey gateway. Go through the gate and walk down to **The Blade**, which is the modern tower with the pointy roof, and then turn left. As the road bends right carry straight on between **Abbots House** and **Abbey Gardens** and you will find the ruins of **Reading Abbey** ahead and left, which also adjoins **HM Prison Reading** which closed in 2013. Its most famous resident is of course Oscar Wilde, who wrote *The Ballad of Reading Gaol* based on the memory of an execution that took place here while he was serving a sentence for homosexual offences.

6 Follow a footpath sign down to Abbey Wharf on the River Kennet and head along the riverside path, through a gate, with an image of Oscar Wilde, and follow the right path under the bridge. Carry on along the towpath, past **Chocolate Island** with a statue of a fisherman, until the path takes you up to the road. *The statue was erected in 1992 opposite the old Huntley & Palmers building when the factory closed and represents a well-known local fisherman who worked there.* Turn left here to visit the **Riverside Museum**, but to continue the walk turn right, over the bridge and follow this road along to a main road. If you've parked in the **Queen's Road car park** turn right and follow the road round to the left to cross over the river. Once over the river take the second right onto **Queen's Road** and back to your car. If you are heading back to the pub turn left onto the main road and cross the bridge over the canal. Then at the end of the bridge turn left down some steps to the towpath. Keep walking on the towpath and you will soon arrive back at the **Fisherman's Cottage**.

Places of Interest

There is a lot to see and do in Reading but highlights include a visit to **Reading Abbey**, which was built at the behest of King Henry I, although he had died by the time it was officially opened by Thomas Becket in 1164. The Abbey was the fourth largest church in Britain. It was such a large and ornate construction that building continued for almost 200 years after the original foundation in 1121.

The **Riverside Museum** contains information about the history of human activity on the Kennet and the Thames rivers in Reading and often hosts art exhibitions and special events.
⊕ readingmuseum.org.uk.

Walk 14
TWYFORD

Distance: 4¼ miles (7 km)

Map: OS Explorer 159 Reading, Wokingham & Pangbourne
Grid Ref: SU787759

How to get there: From the west, leave the M4 at junction 11 and follow signs to Earley, then Sonning, then Twyford and you will see the pub on the right as you enter the town.

From the east, leave the M4 at junction 8/9 and take the A404 up to junction 9b then head west on the A4 until you see a sign for Twyford – drive through the centre of town and straight on at the lights and the pub will be on the left. **Sat Nav:** RG10 9AG.

Parking: The Duke of Wellington has a small car park, which is shared with the library, but there is a pay and display opposite.

This beautiful walk starts on a winding path through Loddon Nature Reserve which is teeming with aquatic birds and insects, such as butterflies, damselflies and dragonflies. The rest of the walk follows some lovely paths and open fields.

THE PUB THE DUKE OF WELLINGTON is a cosy, family and dog friendly pub. It is popular with locals and they host lots of regular events including the annual Twyfest. There is a terraced beer garden with plenty of tables, and a lower garden with more tables and  a children's mini playground. The menu is mostly classic pub grub, but tasty and very reasonably priced.

🌐 thedukeofwellingtontwyford.co.uk ☎ 0118 934 0456

THE WAGGON & HORSES is a little further up the road and also has a large child-friendly beer garden. It is well reviewed by customers and has the advantage of a much larger car park. If you choose to use this pub start the walk by turning right out of the pub. The walk will be about ¼ mile longer.

🌐 No website ☎ 0118 934 0376

The Walk

❶ Turn left out of the **Duke of Wellington** pub and walk along the pavement, over the railway bridge, for about 100 metres until you see a footpath sign (also signed to **Nature Reserve** and **Dinton Pastures**) pointing left. Walk on the gravel path up to a road and carefully cross over, following another **Nature Reserve** sign, over a bridge and then left. Follow the path over a concrete bridge and to the left. Keep on this lovely winding path, with the **River Loddon** to your left, until it ends at a larger path.

❷ Turn left on this path, with the lake on your right. Continue until just after a viewing area where you will see a public footpath sign pointing left. Follow this path under the railway bridge and straight on, with a private fishing lake on your right initially until you reach a small road. Turn left and you will see a public bridleway sign. Shortly afterwards follow a path that forks right

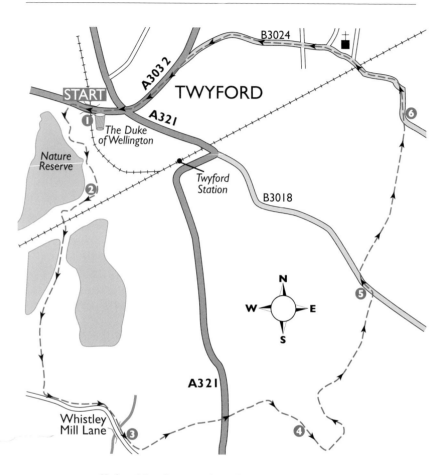

to run parallel with the road. When this path ends, another bridleway sign points you to a path on the other side of the road. Follow this path around to again run parallel with the road – this path can have quite a number of nettles along it at certain times of the year, but you can avoid it by just turning right on the road instead.

3 When the path ends back at the road turn left and follow the road over a bridge. Shortly afterwards you will see a public bridleway sign pointing left, follow this path and at a junction you can take either path as they both go to the same place, but straight on is shorter. When you come to a main road carefully cross over and you will see a byway and a footpath sign – you can take either as they run parallel to each other, the byway is a tree-lined path and the footpath follows the edge of two fields.

4 The paths converge at a wooden bridge after which continue on the byway until you see a footpath sign pointing left. Follow this straight across the field to a metal bridge at the far side, then follow the yellow arrow into woods and at a junction bear left. Follow this occasionally muddy woodland path along to a stile then turn right to follow the right-hand edge of the field (which had little white ponies in at the time of writing). At the end of this field go through a gap into the next field and follow the clear path under a large tree (which sometimes has a rope swing) to a stile at the far end.

5 Cross the stile and turn left onto the pavement of the road. Cross over when you can and after less than 100 metres you will see a footpath sign pointing you through a kissing gate and diagonally across a field. Go through two kissing gates, with a good view of **Stanlake Manor** on your right, and carry on in the same direction along a path between fences, through another kissing gate and straight across the field. Exit the field onto a lane and turn left.

6 Stay on the lane until you cross over the railway bridge and come to a junction opposite **St James the Great church**. Turn left onto the small road which takes you to the main road. Cross over and continue in the same direction along the pavement of the road. Go past **Buratta's** at **The Royal Oak** and cross over. Carry straight on at the next junction and the same again at the traffic lights, then you will shortly arrive back at **The Duke of Wellington** (or keep going another 200 metres for **The Waggon & Horses**).

Places of Interest

Loddon Nature Reserve is a large flooded gravel pit with several islands. It has ideal conditions for wintering birds such as gadwall, smew, tufted duck, pochard, cormorant and snipe. Also be on the lookout for nesting wetland birds such as great crested grebe, moorhen and coot. Herons can often be seen waiting for fish to spear.

Walk 15

WHITE WALTHAM

Distance: 4¼ miles (7 km)

Map: OS Explorer 160 Windsor, Weybridge & Bracknell
Grid Ref: SU849772

How to get there: From the M4 leave at Junction 8/9 and take
the A404(M), leave at the first exit (signposted White Waltham)
and keep following signs for White Waltham until you're in the
village. Keep on the main road and The Beehive will be on your
left. Sat Nav: SL6 3SH.

Parking: The pub has a car park for patrons. Alternatively, you
could park at the cricket club opposite.

This is a nice stroll from the pretty village of White Waltham
through tree-lined paths and fields to the equally lovely village
of Waltham St Lawrence and back again. The pub is easy to find
and the walk is completely flat so should be suitable for all. This
is a good walk for blackberry picking during late summer. One
path can get a bit overgrown with nettles and brambles so shorts
are probably not advisable.

THE PUB THE BEEHIVE is a very attractive family-run pub and restaurant which has long been a popular destination in these parts. The service is very friendly, and the British menu is seasonal.

⊕ thebeehivewhitewaltham.com ☎ 01628 822877

THE BELL in Waltham St Lawrence (at point 6 on the walk) is a good alternative if you'd prefer a lunchtime soup or sandwich.

⊕ thebellwalthamstlawrence.co.uk ☎ 0118 934 1788

The Walk

1 Turn right out of **The Beehive car park** and head along the pavement for about 100 metres. Cross over briefly onto **Butcher's Lane**, and then turn left following the public footpath sign past the **First and Second World War memorial**. Walk across the edge of the cricket pitch towards a gap in the fence at the back. Go through the gap and turn right on the narrow path along to a stile. Cross the stile and head straight across the field, heading to the right of a pond and towards the church.

2 Just before you reach the church turn left onto a concrete path, but as the path bears left keep going straight on, following the line of the trees on your right, heading towards a stile next to a metal gate. Cross the stile and walk along a short path to a gate and onto the road. Turn right briefly on the road and then cross over and head down the gravel track opposite. Follow this path as it bears slightly right and along to a gate that looks like a dead end, but to the right is a stile to cross into the field.

3 Turn left and head across the field on a clear path towards a stile at the far corner. Cross the stile and go straight on along a path

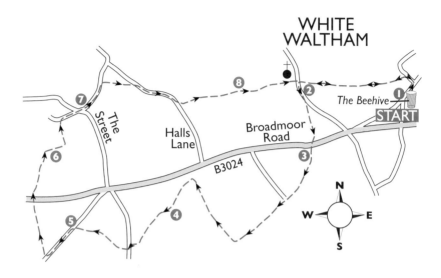

between fences. At a crossroads of paths turn right along another narrow path to a large metal kissing gate. Cross a meadow and head into the trees at the far side and straight on through another two kissing gates. When you come to a concrete path head left on the restricted byway and once you've reached the static caravans on your right, look left for a stile with a public footpath sign.

4 Cross into the field and proceed along its right edge, and then onto a path through the bushes, which will take you along to another kissing gate. Go through the gate, along a clear path and through another gate onto the road. Head left briefly then cross to a public footpath sign pointing right to a gate. Follow this often slightly overgrown path between a stream and a fence to another wooden gate and exit onto the road and turn left onto the pavement.

5 Walk for about 200 metres until just before the 30mph sign. You will see a public footpath sign on the right pointing you through a kissing gate and into a field. Go diagonally right across the field on a clear path which eventually joins up with some deeply rutted tyre tracks. This takes you along to a kissing gate next to a large metal gate. Head left briefly on the road then cross to a public footpath sign pointing right. Go through a gate into a field and bear slightly right to pass between two white posts, then head for some more posts in the far right corner of the field.

6 Go through a kissing gate and over a small bridge to head along the right edge of the field, keeping right around a corner. After about 50 metres you should see a path heading directly left. Follow this path straight across the field to a junction of footpaths. Take the right-hand path into a cul-de-sac and follow the road down to the main road. Turn right towards **The Bell** pub then head to the left on the road (**Halls Lane**) between the pub and the church.

7 Walk along the road for about 100 metres until you see a public footpath sign to the right, follow this path, straight across a drive, until you reach a gravel track with a burial ground on the right. Turn left down the track to the road and turn right for about 200 metres until you see footpath signs heading left and right. Take the left path across a stile and along the right edge of a field, through some woods and along to a stile to the right.

8 Cross the stile and follow the left edge of the next field into some trees, and along to a brick archway. Continue straight on, past the church on your left and through a kissing gate. Go straight on across the field you should recognise from the start of the walk and retrace your steps back to the cricket pitch, where you can turn right instead of left and head between the nets and the clubhouse to the car park, then left back to the pub.

Places of Interest

Waltham St Lawrence has roots in Saxon times and even had an unusual hexagonal Romano-English temple, which can apparently be seen from aerial photographs. The Saxons destroyed the original settlement in the 7th century and **Waltham** comes from the Saxon meaning unsteady house or home. The **St Lawrence** bit comes from the name of the church, which is of considerable antiquity, with some traces of pre-13th-century work in the crude Norman arches at the west end of the nave.

Walk 16
COOKHAM

Distance: 3¾ miles (6 km)

Map: OS Explorer 172 Chiltern Hills East **Grid Ref:** SU897855

How to get there: From the M4 leave at Junction 8/9 and take the A308(M) towards Maidenhead, then turn left at the roundabout and follow the dual carriageway until it meets the A4. Turn right towards Slough and keep going until you see a sign on the left for Cookham. Follow this road all the way into Cookham and keep going until you see The Ferry on your right. **Sat Nav:** SL6 9SN.

Parking: The pub has a car park but it does get busy. If you're doing a pre-lunch walk you should be fine. Alternatively, there is some roadside parking in the village or a car park on Sutton Road which is ¼ mile from the pub.

Not many walks include a spot where one could paddle - or even swim - in the river on a hot day. This one does. The first half is spent following a lovely stretch of the Thames, during which you'll pass an alternative riverside pub (with a mini playground in the beer garden), while the return leg takes you along pleasant country paths. You pass a further three pubs while heading back into Cookham, but the riverside setting of The Ferry makes it well worth waiting for!

THE PUB THE FERRY is quite a large pub, with two floors of seating and a patio next to the River Thames. It's worth booking as it gets pretty full and it's easy to see why. Not only is the setting wonderful, but the food is too, and on the busy Sunday lunchtime when I visited, the service was still prompt as well. The menus are extensive and imaginative, with a separate kids' and vegan menu. During the week the lunch menu also extends to pizzas, sandwiches and salads along with some enticing house specials.
🌐 theferry.co.uk ☎ 01628 525123

The Walk

1 From the pub car park walk up a short set of steps to the road, carefully cross straight over, and go down some steps opposite. Turn right onto an alley between buildings. At the end of the alley turn left onto the riverside path. After a short distance there is a jetty where you can catch a steamer to **Marlow** or **Windsor**, but only on a Monday. Carry on through a couple of gates past **Cookham Sailing Club**.

2 Stay on the **Thames Path** with fields on your left and go through a metal kissing gate passing a spot with a mini beach where people can paddle. Go through a couple of gates to pass under the railway bridge. (The **Thames Path** crosses over the bridge at this point, and then passes a friendly looking pub called **The Bounty**.) Go through a large wooden kissing gate and then through a metal one and continue on the path as it finally diverges from the **Thames**.

3 At the apex of the fence you will see a footpath sign pointing left straight across a field, follow this to a small wooden gate next to a large metal one. Go through and along to a junction of footpaths where you turn left on the lower path that follows the bottom of the hill.

4 When the path ascends slightly go through a gate and then when it forks keep left to go through another gate and then under the railway arch. Go over the cattle grid (or through the small gate next to it), then turn right on a path that runs alongside a golf course. You can see the riverside path from earlier on here and if you want to take a short cut just head across and retrace your steps to the start. Otherwise,

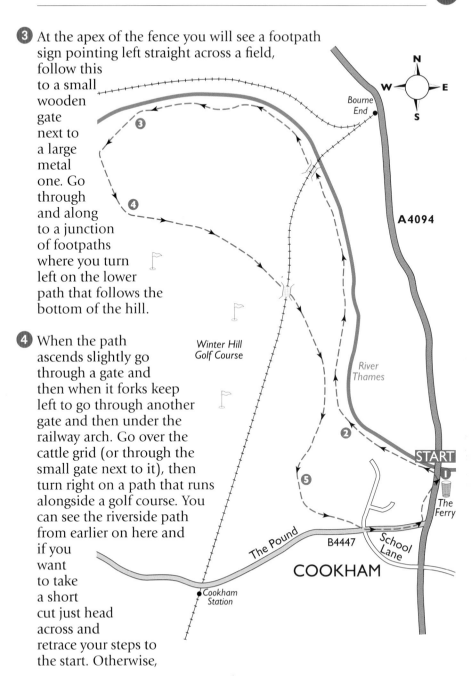

Bourne End

A4094

Winter Hill
Golf Course

River
Thames

START

The
Ferry

The Pound

B4447

School
Lane

COOKHAM

Cookham
Station

stay on this path until a track running alongside you on the right bears right and your path bears slightly left.

5 Continue with the path bearing left through a small gate and over a little bridge, then across the end of a car park and straight on along the left edge of a field until you pass **The Crown** pub on your left and join the main road. Stay on the left pavement going through the centre of **Cookham**, past more pubs, and when you pass the **Stanley Spencer Gallery** on your right follow the road around to the left, cross over carefully and follow the pavement back to **The Ferry**.

Places of Interest

Cookham is well known for its association with the artist Stanley Spencer. He was born and raised in Cookham and was extremely attached to the place, describing it as 'a village in heaven'. Many of his works are on display in the **Stanley Spencer Gallery** in the village. Check the website for opening times.
⊕ stanleyspencer.org.uk.

Walk 17

ARBORFIELD CROSS

Distance: 3¾ miles (6 km)

Map: OS Explorer 159 Reading, Wokingham & Pangbourne
Grid Ref: SU761670

How to get there: From the M4, leave at junction 11 and follow signs for Earley, taking you east next to the M4. At the roundabout turn right, over the M4, and follow signs for Arborfield until you come to The Bull Inn on the right, just before a large roundabout. **Sat Nav:** RG2 9QD.

Parking: The Bull Inn has a large car park. There is also some roadside parking opposite the pub on Swallowfield Road.

This is a pleasant and easy to follow walk. It is almost completely flat and the footpaths are wide (apart from one near the end) and well signposted. The first half is wooded and the second is a mixture of open and tree-lined paths. There are two villages to explore, Arborfield and Arborfield Cross, although it's difficult to know where one starts and the other finishes. The cross actually refers to the junction (now a roundabout) on which The Bull Inn is situated.

THE PUB

THE BULL INN, although situated next to a largish roundabout, has a fairly secluded beer garden at the rear with a grassy area for children to play. Inside, the pub is geared towards dining, but the prices are more reasonable than many. The staff are friendly and the cuisine is a mixture of pub staples, with a sprinkling of international dishes and includes a lighter lunchtime menu.

🌐 thebullinnarborfield.co.uk ☎ 0118 976 2244

The Walk

1 Make your way to the opposite side of the large roundabout where you'll see a byway sign pointing away from the roundabout. Follow this broad track, for about 600 metres, down to a little bridge over a stream. Carry on in the same direction past a byway called **School Road**, staying on **Bearwood Road** at the next well signposted junction. Go past **Wysipig Farm Shop** and then straight on at the next junction. After about 300 metres you will see a wooden gate/barrier on the left, just before a junction of paths ahead. Turn left here.

2 Follow the path next to the golf course, ignoring the smaller path branching left, until the path winds its way back to the broad track, where you turn right. Follow the track along to a road. Cross over and continue on the gravel byway opposite. This track ends at a small lane. Turn left, then left again following the byway sign down a gravel track to a bridge to the left of a ford. Go over the bridge and carry on along the winding path until you reach a junction of footpaths to the right and byway straight on. Go straight on.

3 Stay on this nice tree-lined path all the way to a road. Turn right for less than 100 metres and then left following a public footpath sign (ignoring the '**Private Property**' sign) and another footpath

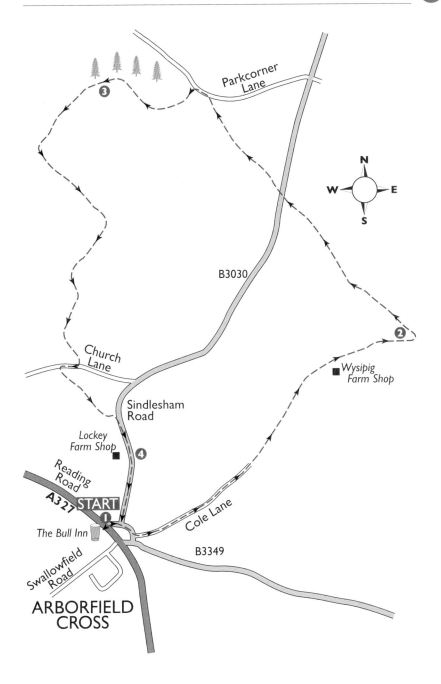

sign pointing between fences. Follow this narrow path until it ends at a road. Carefully turn right here, initially on the right-hand side of the road. After about 50 metres carefully cross over to where there is a wider verge to walk on.

4 After another few hundred metres, opposite **Lockey Farm Shop and Butchers**, follow a footpath on the left-hand side of the road and after that there is a pavement. As you approach the roundabout cross over and cut across a patch of green towards **The Bull Inn**. Cross the road carefully back to the pub.

Places of Interest

Just 5 miles away is **Dinton Pastures Country Park** where you can hire boats, go fishing or enjoy the award-winning kids' play park, where you'll find swings, a willow maze and secret hobbit holes. There is also a café selling a good range of lunchtime options and homemade cakes. ⊕ dinton-pastures.co.uk

Walk 18
FINCHAMPSTEAD

Distance: 4¼ miles (7 km)

Map: OS Explorer 159 Reading, Wokingham & Pangbourne
Grid Ref: SU793639

How to get there: From the M4, leave at junction 11 and follow signs for Earley, taking you east next to the M4, then at the roundabout turn right, over the M4, and follow signs for Arborfield until you come to a large roundabout. Take the 3rd exit, signposted Farnborough and Aldershot, then keep following these signs until you enter a village signposted Finchampstead at the end of which is a turning to the left, signposted Finchampstead. Follow this road until you see a small road on the left signposted for the church. Follow this road and you can't miss the pub next to the church. **Sat Nav:** RG40 4LS.

Parking: The Queen's Oak has a decent-sized car park. Alternatively, there is parking by the church.

Starting on lovely tree-lined paths through Finchampstead, this walk then takes you down to the River Blackwater, along the Blackwater Valley Path and the Moor Green Lakes Nature Reserve. The Blackwater Valley has been subject to an improvement programme, and as a result much wildlife is returning to the area, including otters, which had been absent for 40 years. The Moor Green Lakes Nature Reserve was created following 50 years of gravel extraction, and the birds have flocked in as a result.

THE QUEEN'S OAK is a classic country pub. It's cosy inside with a nice beer garden to the side, and lots of activities in the evenings. The food is good with a selection of pizzas (and baguettes on weekdays) on top of the more traditional sort of offerings.

⊕ thequeensoak.com ☎ 0118 996 8567

The Walk

1 Opposite the pub, towards the church, there is an information board and next to that is a footpath sign with orange and yellow arrows. Follow that and then a few metres later there is another sign with arrows pointing straight on and slightly right. Go straight on up the slope towards the church and then go into the churchyard and walk around the back of the church. Head down the hill, forking slightly right, then straight on and through a gate and down to a junction of footpaths where you turn right.

2 Follow this lovely tree-lined path (which can get muddy at times) as it bears left, then right, over a bridge and through a gate, and

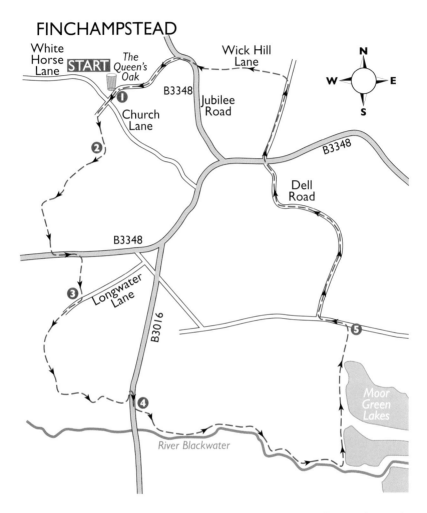

along to a junction of footpaths where you turn left. Go through the gate and keep on in the same direction along a tarmac drive and down to a main road. Turn left onto the pavement and carefully cross over the road before the petrol station. You should see a footpath sign pointing off to the right, follow this wooded path straight on until it ends at a junction.

3 Turn right on a gravel track and carry straight on when the drive bears left. This path can get quite muddy, but there are wooden

stepping stones at the more tricky bits. At the junction of paths carry straight on and then go through a gate and over a bridge. At the next junction turn left over the bridge and through a gate. Follow this lovely path past a lake and bear left at a junction, following the blue arrow for 'Blackwater Valley Way'. Go through a kissing gate and along to the road then cross over to a footpath opposite.

4 Follow this path as it winds along to join another path, where you go straight on with the **River Blackwater** to your right and, at the time of writing, some quarrying on your left. After about ¾ mile go through a couple of gates to cross a track, then a few hundred metres later you'll come to a junction with two parallel paths heading left. Take the 2nd path as it has better views of the **Moor Green Lakes** (both paths lead to the same place). The paths converge to cross a bridge, then diverge, and again the right fork is nicer.

5 The path ends at a car park. Turn left on the quiet road for about 150 metres, then right onto **Dell Road**. Follow this quiet lane for about ¾ mile as it winds uphill to a larger road, then cross over and proceed along the bridleway opposite. After about 300 metres an unmarked track heads left, follow this (the sign saying private road only applies to vehicles, it is a bridleway) down to a road. Cross over the road and turn right onto the pavement. You will soon come across a turning on the left with a sign for the **Queen's Oak**. Follow this quiet road back to the pub.

Places of Interest

California Country Park is less than two miles north of the pub and is a great place to explore. The 100-acre country park has a lake, a children's play park with a pirate ship and plenty of nature trails to follow. It is open every day and there is also a café and a paddling pool during the summer months.

Walk 19
WOKINGHAM

Distance: 3½ miles (5.75 km)

Map: OS Explorer 159 Reading, Wokingham & Pangbourne
Grid Ref: SU826667

How to get there: From the M4 leave at Junction 10 and take the A329(M) towards Bracknell, then just after it stops being a motorway turn right at the first roundabout (signposted 'Local Routes') then right again and straight on at the next roundabout. Follow the road around to the left past a turning on the right for Wokingham, then after about ¾ mile look out for a small turning on the right, again for Wokingham. Take this road and the first turning on the left takes you straight to the pub but the road is narrow and you have to cross a ford. So, take the second left, just before another pub, and then left again on Honey Hill and you will arrive at the pub. **Sat Nav:** RG40 3BJ.

Parking: The pub has two car parks; a larger one on the right and an overflow one on the left, the walk starts from the overflow car park.

This lovely countryside walk is easy to follow and mostly flat. The tree-lined paths make the route shady in parts, so it is perfect for a hot day. At the right time of year this walk would be good for blackberry picking. If you have time it's also worth visiting Holme Grange Craft Village (see Places of Interest section) and picking up some locally made gifts.

THE CROOKED BILLET looks quite modern from the outside with pristine white clapperboards all around, but inside it is cosy with oak beams and nooks with paraphernalia along with book cases making it quite charming. There is also a pleasant beer garden to the side and benches at the front. The food is good with a wide array of options including a nice selection of sandwiches and a Grazing Menu, which has about 20 small dishes to either snack on or to make a tapas-style lunch.
⊕ crookedbilletwokingham.co.uk ☎ 0118 978 0438

The Walk

1 At the far right-hand corner of the overflow car park go through a large open gate and proceed past undercover crops on your right. Turn right and then left to skirt around the craft village car park heading along a gravel track towards the road. Turn right along the verge of the road for about 50 metres until you come to a somewhat faded footpath sign pointing left.

2 Cross the road carefully and head up the drive towards Grays Farm Pick Your Own and Farm Shop. Keep going past the farm then as you bear slightly left you will see another footpath sign keeping you going in pretty much the same direction. After you have passed the crops on your right and a picnic area you will see footpath signs pointing left and right. Go right on the path between the PYO and a small golf course. At the end of the golf course the footpath forks slightly left onto a lovely tree-lined path.

3 Keep going straight on over a small road. Just before a bridge you'll see a footpath sign pointing left. Go over a stile and along to a bridge with barriers at either end and keep going straight on through a couple of wooden gate/barriers onto another path

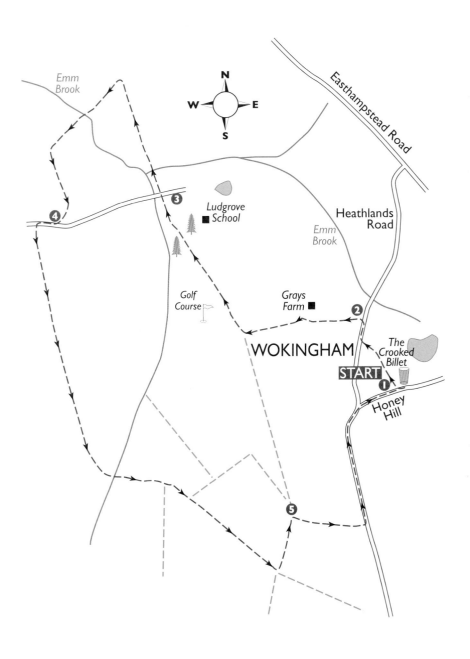

Emm
Brook

N
W
E
S

3
Ludgrove
■ School

4

Heathlands
Road

Emm
Brook

Golf
Course

Grays
Farm ■

2

WOKINGHAM

The
Crooked
Billet

START 1

Honey
Hill

5

where you turn left. Go through another barrier and straight on onto a lane. When the lane bears right go straight on along the path that then bears right.

4 Follow the path to a road and turn right to a road junction with a byway sign pointing left. Follow this and proceed along this long straight lane, which occasionally has vehicles, for about ¾ mile until it bears slightly left and you pass between a car park and a campsite. Go straight on along a track through a plantation. After the campsite and a further 500 metres, as the path bears slightly left, you will see paths going off to either side, head left on a small path into the woods.

5 At a junction of footpaths turn right along a narrow woodland path and follow this occasionally muddy path all the way to a road. Turn left on the verge of the road, past the garden centre, and on until you see Honey Hill heading off to the right. Follow this lane back to the pub.

Places of Interest

Holme Grange Craft Village offers a wide range of products including jewellery and sweets made by a number of local independent traders and artisan crafters all working in a series of converted barns. There is also a large free car park and a good café. ⊕ holmegrangecraftvillage.co.uk

Grays Farm Pick Your Own and Farm Shop is also worth a visit and is open between May and October.⊕ graysfarm.co.uk

Walk 20

BRACKNELL

Distance: 4 miles (6.4 km)

Map: OS Explorer 160 Windsor, Weybridge & Bracknell
Grid Ref: SU854660

How to get there: From the M4 leave at Junction 10 and take the A329(M) towards Bracknell, then just after it stops being a motorway turn right at the first roundabout (signposted 'Local Routes') then right again and straight on at the next roundabout. Follow the road around to the left, then at the next roundabout turn left towards Bracknell and the pub is about a mile along on the right. **Sat Nav:** RG40 3DR.

Parking: The pub has a good-sized car park but please ask the landlord's permission before leaving your car.

This is a lovely walk through part of Swinley Forest, which is owned and run by the Crown Estate. This 2600-acre forest is where some of *Harry Potter and the Deathly Hallows* was filmed and is also popular with mountain bikers. On the route you will pass through an Iron Age hillfort, walk a small section of the Three Castles Path and the part of the Devil's Highway.

THE PUB THE GOLDEN RETRIEVER is a large thatched pub with lots of character and charm. They serve good food at reasonable prices, with a fixed-price weekday menu, a vegan menu and a selection of lighter lunches which include pizzas and sandwiches. There is plenty of room inside and a terrace in front, but it's a popular pub and can get pretty busy, so booking might be advisable.
⊕ vintageinn.co.uk ☎ 01344 868535

The Walk

① From the pub car park turn right onto the main road. Cross over at the crossing, and then cross carefully over **Crowthorne Road**. Turn right onto the pavement to head in the direction signposted to **Coral Reef Waterworld**. After about 50 metres the pavement ends and a footpath and ramblers route sign will point you left into the woods. Shortly after, turn right following the ramblers route sign again. Follow this path, parallel to the road, over a bridge and up a small hill, for nearly ½ mile until, just after you see a signpost saying **Orion**, you see a public right of way sign on the right leading to the main road.

② Cross carefully over the road and take the byway opposite into **Swinley Forest**. Head towards the information board about **Caesar's Camp** and go straight past it, through a kissing gate, and into the hillfort. Go straight on, up the hill, along a path that gradually curves to the left, and carry straight on into open scrubland as another path joins from the left. Keep going on this path until you pass through another kissing gate to a large junction of footpaths.

③ Turn left, signposted towards **The Look Out**. Go straight on past a crossing path and down the hill, passing a pond on your right, to another junction of four paths. Take the rightmost path up the hill. Ignore the first path on your right, then after you have crested the hill take the next right on a broad gravel path with

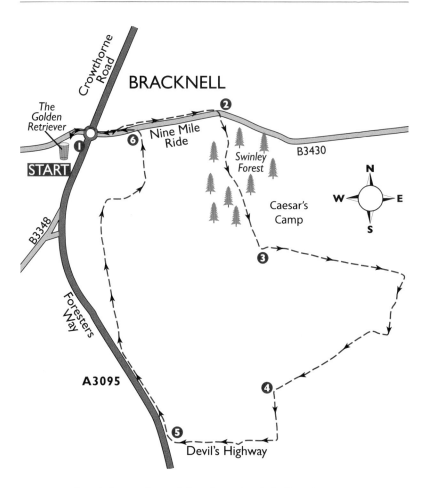

trees to the right and scrubland to the left for about 50 metres, then fork left. At the next crossroads go straight on, under the cables, this time with trees to your left. Keep going until the path ends at a T-junction.

4 Turn left following a brown arrow, and soon you will reach another crossroads where you turn right along the **Devil's Highway** (note the red flag straight ahead which indicates the start of the 'Danger Area'). Go down the hill, past a green gate, on a restricted byway, then just as the road bridge comes into view take a path that forks off to the right between two fences.

5 Follow this path parallel to the road then bear right. Cross over a stile, then fork left (on a path that's not on the OS map). Stay on this path, which also stays parallel to the road, ignoring offshoots to the right, until the path bends slightly to the right, and then keep straight on up **Hut Hill** and down the other side. The path ends at a junction of paths. Take the path roughly opposite and follow it around to the right to a five-way junction where you continue around to the left (or 2nd path on the left).

6 When the path approaches the road bear left with it, next to the road. Then, as it forks away from the road, turn right and cross carefully to the pavement. Turn left and retrace your steps back to the pub.

Places of Interest

A few miles away is **The Look Out Discovery Centre**, a hands-on science and nature exhibition with over 90 activities to keep your children entertained, including an insect enclosure and indoor stream.

⊕ bracknell-forest.gov.uk/leisure-services/look-out-discovery-centre

OTHER TITLES FROM COUNTRYSIDE BOOKS

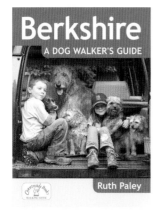

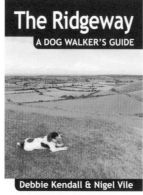

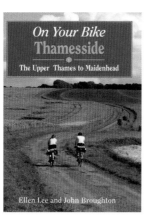

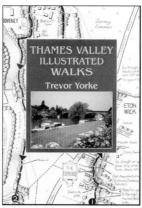

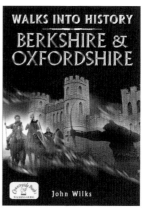

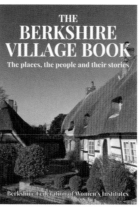

To see the full range of books by Countryside Books please visit
www.countrysidebooks.co.uk

Follow us on   @CountrysideBooks